TO

_____

FROM

_____

"Transformation starts in the home, and Bill and Beni Johnson model that truth so well. Their new book will charge your faith as your whole family comes together to practice the Word of God and partner with His will for your lives!"

DR. CHÉ AHN, founder and president, Harvest International Ministry; founding and senior pastor, Harvest Rock Church, Pasadena, California; international chancellor, Wagner University; founder, Ché Ahn Ministries

"Every believing parent wants to 'train up a child in the way he should go,' but too often, we focus most of our attention on teaching our children all the ways they shouldn't go. That's where this book differs from most. It equips parents to lead their children with a God-given vision. It facilitates a deep relationship with God and each other like few books can. With the short teachings, meditations, prayers and instructions on what we can do with our kids, Bill and Beni Johnson impart their family legacy into ours. To me, that makes this book a priceless addition to any home."

SETH AND LAUREN DAHL, authors, *Raising Spirit-Led Kids* and *Win+Win Parenting*

"When I read *Bible Promises and Prayers for Children*, I thought immediately of a current literary device several prominent people are using: Letters to My Younger Self. I would have loved to have this guide when we were raising our blended family."

BISHOP JOSEPH L. GARLINGTON SR.,
founding pastor, Covenant Church of Pittsburgh

"A family with a legacy rich in relationship with God often has origins of devotion that began at home. *Bible Promises and Prayers for Children* intimately fosters revival, relationship and a hunger for God's presence in ways that are transformative to the DNA of the whole family! This book is a must-have for every household."

KRIS VALLOTTON, leader, Bethel Church, Redding, California; co-founder, Bethel School of Supernatural Ministry; author, *The Supernatural Ways of Royalty, Spirit Wars, Heavy Rain* and more

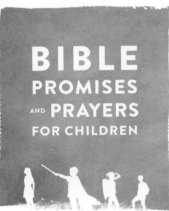

BIBLE
PROMISES
AND PRAYERS
FOR CHILDREN

BIBLE
PROMISES
AND PRAYERS
FOR CHILDREN

RELEASING YOUR CHILD'S
DIVINE DESTINY

BILL and **BENI JOHNSON**
with ABIGAIL McKOY

Chosen
a division of Baker Publishing Group
Minneapolis, Minnesota

© 2021 by BRevived, LLC

Published by Chosen Books
11400 Hampshire Avenue South
Bloomington, Minnesota 55438
www.chosenbooks.com

Chosen Books is a division of
Baker Publishing Group, Grand Rapids, Michigan

Printed in China

ISBN 978-0-8007-6212-4

Library of Congress Control Number: 2020944911

Unless otherwise indicated, Scripture quotations are from The Passion Translation®. Copyright © 2017, 2018 by Passion & Fire Ministries, Inc. Used by permission. All rights reserved. ThePassionTranslation.com.

Scripture quotations identified AMP are from the Amplified® Bible (AMP), copyright © 2015 by The Lockman Foundation. Used by permission. www.Lockman.org

Scripture quotations identified MESSAGE are taken from *THE MESSAGE*, copyright © 1993, 2002, 2018 by Eugene H. Peterson. Used by permission of NavPress. All rights reserved. Represented by Tyndale House Publishers, Inc.

Scripture quotations identified NASB are from the New American Standard Bible® (NASB), copyright © 1960, 1962, 1963, 1968, 1971, 1972, 1973, 1975, 1977, 1995 by The Lockman Foundation. Used by permission. www.Lockman.org

Scripture quotations identified NIV are from THE HOLY BIBLE, NEW INTERNATIONAL VERSION®, NIV® Copyright © 1973, 1978, 1984, 2011 by Biblica, Inc.® Used by permission. All rights reserved worldwide.

Scripture quotations identified NKJV are from the New King James Version®. Copyright © 1982 by Thomas Nelson. Used by permission. All rights reserved.

Scripture quotations identified NLT are taken from the Holy Bible, New Living Translation, copyright © 1996, 2004, 2015 by Tyndale House Foundation. Used by permission of Tyndale House Publishers, Inc., Carol Stream, Illinois 60188. All rights reserved.

Cover design by LOOK Design Studio
Interior design by William Overbeeke

21 22 23 24 25 26 27   7 6 5 4 3 2 1

May our sons flourish in their youth
   like well-nurtured plants.
May our daughters be like graceful pillars,
   carved to beautify a palace.
May our barns be filled
   with crops of every kind.
May the flocks in our fields multiply by the
      thousands,
   even tens of thousands,
   and may our oxen be loaded down with
      produce.
May there be no enemy breaking through
      our walls,
   no going into captivity,
   no cries of alarm in our town squares.
Yes, joyful are those who live like this!
Joyful indeed are those whose God is the
      LORD.

Psalm 144:12–15 NLT

CONTENTS

Your Child Is a Treasure

Each child is a gift from God that we—parents, grandparents and caregivers—are commanded to treasure. This is both our greatest joy and our most sober responsibility. In light of this, *Bible Promises and Prayers for Children* is intended to nourish you, as well as the children in your care. Each entry begins with a short teaching message, includes related Scripture to meditate on and concludes with a guided prayer. Beni and I hope that reading this book will become a time of encouragement as you connect to God's heart for your family and beyond.

In each entry, we have also created a section where your children can participate with you. Together, you can discuss the question(s) we offer. Then you can invite your kids to pray with you, make a bold declaration of faith and engage in the suggested activity. Our prayer is that this would provide an opportunity for discovery and connection between your family and your heavenly Father.

May this book lead you and your entire household into encounters with the almighty God so that your family might impact the world with His love, power, wisdom and purity.

Training Up a Child

God focuses His loving attention on those who belong to Him. Hebrews says that "the Lord disciplines the one he loves, and he chastens everyone he accepts as his son" (Hebrews 12:6 NIV). God longs to impart His holiness and peace-filled righteousness to all His children. And He has given us the authority and responsibility to impart identity, character and purpose into the lives of the children in our care.

When we walk kids through healthy discipline, we are investing in them. We are reorienting them into an awareness of why they are alive and into the fullness of their inheritance. But this kind of discipline requires godly wisdom. It needs to be an occasion, not an outburst.

Real discipline takes time. The strength of our discipline comes from our ability to respond to a child rather than reacting to his or her behavior. And that means allowing ourselves to be inconvenienced sometimes.

We all know that children can act out at the most awkward moments—in the grocery store, at a dinner party, in front of guests—and naturally, parents can find themselves either ignoring bad behavior or reacting angrily to put a stop to it. But neither of these produce the fruit we want to see in our children's lives. If we take the time to invest in the moment of discipline, it will spare us much disappointment and pain later.

God's discipline comes from a heart of love, and we model that for our children, shaping their hearts with responsibility and purpose. When we take the time to discuss with them what they did wrong, we are able to make sure they understand their misstep. We give them time to adjust their attitude and take responsibility, and we deliver an appropriate correction if needed.

We get to approach our children with humility and love. Godly discipline is never done out of frustration or vindication, but with tender care. We are raising children to become adults, leaders and parents. Partnering with them for their future success as they grow will impact them for the rest of their lives.

For the Lord's training of your life is the evidence of his faithful love. And when he draws you to himself, it proves you are his delightful child.

Fully embrace God's correction as part of your training, for he is doing what any loving father does for his children. For who has ever heard of a child who never had to be corrected? We all should welcome God's discipline as the validation of authentic sonship. For if we have never once endured his correction it only proves we are strangers and not sons. *Hebrews 12:6–8*

He who spares his rod hates his son, but he who loves him disciplines him promptly. *Proverbs 13:24 NKJV*

You are witnesses, and so is God, how devoutly and uprightly and blamelessly we behaved toward you believers; just as you know how we were exhorting and encouraging and imploring each one of you as a father would his own children, so that you would walk in a manner worthy of the God who calls you into His own kingdom and glory. *1 Thessalonians 2:10–12 NASB*

Lord, fill me with Your faithful love so that when I need to redirect ___, it comes from that tender place. Help me delight in Your discipline in my own life so that I can accurately represent Your heart to ___ when I bring correction. Thank You that You care enough about us to invest in training us in the ways that we should go. Thank You that You mark us with identity when You discipline us. Holy Spirit, help me bring discipline promptly, but patiently. Give me God's wisdom to know when to correct and when to tenderly encourage. Thank You for the destiny that You've given ___, God. Thank You that You are faithful to equip those whom You have called; I will remind ___ of who You have created this child of Yours to be.

FOR TIME WITH
Your CHILD

ASK: How do you feel when you are disciplined? Everyone needs training so they can become their best selves. What areas of your life do you feel as if God is helping you grow in today?

PRAY: *Holy Spirit, remind me how amazing You think I am even when I mess up. Thanks that You always love me the same, no matter what. But help me to keep growing, Jesus, so I can be more like You every day.*

DECLARE: I have a powerful destiny. I am important enough to God that He cares about training me!

DO: What kinds of gifts and talents has God put inside you? Discuss with each other the call of God on your life and what kinds of character attributes you will need to fulfill that calling.

2

Prophesy Their Destiny

One of the core beliefs of the Christian faith is that God still speaks. It would be impossible for us to be born again otherwise. God called us to Himself, and we responded with surrender (see 1 Corinthians 1:9).

God longs to speak to us about our lives, and especially about the lives and destinies of our children and grandchildren. He has specific insight into the design of each child, and learning to hear Him in this way can make all the difference in our homes.

Zechariah prophesied over his son, John the Baptist, when the child was only eight days old (see Luke 1:67–79). The baby was too young to understand consciously what his father was saying, but prophetic words reveal the heart of God. And the heart of God must be declared.

In 1 Corinthians 14:1, we are told to "desire earnestly spiritual gifts, but especially that you may prophesy" (NASB). The point is, not only is it legal to pursue specific gifts of the Holy Spirit, it is commanded. As parents, we need this prophetic gift in a big way. Prophetic insight is essential for raising children.

God has a unique purpose for each child, and we can help our children discover that purpose. The Bible tells us, "Train up a child in the way *he should go*, even when he is old he will not depart from it" (Proverbs 22:6 NASB, emphasis added). The verse says "in the way he should go." It does not say we should train up a child in the way we want him or her to go.

Our job is to plant the seeds in our children's lives, and then cover their lives with prayer. Prayer brings the water, so to speak. And it is God who will bring forth fruit from the seeds we have planted.

Before I formed you in the womb I knew you, before you were born I set you apart. *Jeremiah 1:5 NIV*

"And you, child, will be called the prophet of the Highest; for you will go before the face of the Lord to prepare His ways, to give knowledge of salvation to His people by the remission of their sins, through the tender mercy of our God, with which the Dayspring from on high has visited us; to give light to those who sit in darkness and the shadow of death, to guide our feet into the way of peace." *Luke 1:76–79 NKJV*

"For I know the plans I have for you," declares the LORD, "plans to prosper you and not to harm you, plans to give you hope and a future."

Jeremiah 29:11 NIV

God, I need Your insight into ___'s destiny. I want to speak life, truth and identity over ___. Will You give me a vision for Your plans for ___'s life? Thank You that You have planted gifts, skills, passions and dreams in this child's heart. Help me call those out prophetically so that ___ can walk with confidence the path of life that You have laid out. I need Your wisdom, Lord, to guide me as I empower and correct ___. Help me fan the flames of who ___ is, while providing godly correction. I want to see this child the way You do.

ASK: What do you love to do? Why do you think God might have built you with those specific passions and interests?

PRAY: *Thank You, God, that You created me with special gifts, talents and passions to bring to the world. I will keep listening to who You say that I am!*

DECLARE: God knows every part of me. He has special things to say to me about my life!

DO: What do you think God loves about each person in this room? Take some time to tell each person what you think God would say about him or her.

3

God Is Good

You will not be able to exaggerate God's goodness. You can twist, dilute or redefine it, but He is better than any of us think. And because of this, we must change the way that we think and speak to our children about this foundational attribute of the Lord's goodness.

Scripture says God is good, so we must believe it. But then, why do bad things happen? Throughout history, people have credited God with many horrible wars, natural disasters and diseases because of His omnipotence and the idea that He is in control of everything. Although it is true that He is in charge, it is not true that He is in control. God designed the infrastructure of the world to include our free will, and our choices about things affect the outcome.

For example, Scripture tells us that God is "not willing that any should perish but that all should come to repentance" (2 Peter 3:9 NKJV). Are people perishing? Yes. Is it His will? No. He gives each person the free will to choose his or her eternal outcome.

As parents and grandparents, we should be able to relate to this particular distinction between God being in charge and God taking control. We are in charge of our homes, but we are not always in control over everything that happens there.

God has written us into His plan as co-laborers for His Kingdom. In this context, our children must learn how to explore the depth of God's goodness and dream big. Because He has invited us to partner with Him creatively on the earth, we have an obligation to pursue God-sized dreams that only He can fulfill. You are helping raise a generation who will know God as such a good Father that they will dream with confidence about the redemption of the world.

Because Jesus called His disciples friends, He invited them to ask whatever they wanted of Him (see John 14:13). This was not an invitation to selfishness or greed; it was an acknowledgment that their hearts were so connected with His that He wanted to co-labor with them to see heaven come to earth. This is the mindset—set on the foundation of God's goodness—that we want our children to inherit.

Give thanks to the LORD, for he is good; his love endures forever. *Psalm 107:1 NIV*

Everything we could ever need for life and complete devotion to God has already been deposited in us by his divine power. For all this was lavished upon us through the rich experience of knowing him who has called us by name and invited us to come to him through a glorious manifestation of his goodness. *2 Peter 1:3*

Oh, taste and see that the LORD is good; blessed is the man who trusts in Him! *Psalm 34:8 NKJV*

God, thank You that Your goodness is integral to who You are. Thank You that we can trust that Your goodness and love are wrapped around us at every moment. You have invited ___ to experience Your goodness daily and learn to trust Your heart. Help ___ receive Your love and mercy, pursue Your heart and explore the realms of Your goodness past where I have gone. Help ___ dream huge, God-sized dreams with You, Father.

FOR TIME WITH
Your CHILD

ASK: Jesus only did what the Father told Him to do. What kinds of things can you see in Jesus' life that reveal God's goodness?

PRAY: *God, thank You for being such a good, good Father to me. I want to become more aware of Your goodness every day. Holy Spirit, would You remind me of God's goodness whenever I forget?*

DECLARE: God's goodness is extravagant, and it is pointed right at me!

DO: Take some time to talk about some personal testimonies of God's goodness. Build your faith together as you see what God is able and wanting to do.

4

Nothing Is Impossible

In the gospel of Luke, an angel of the Lord tells Mary that she will give birth to the Son of God. Unsure how that could happen since she is still a virgin, Mary questions the angel. The angel responds by sharing a prophecy about Elizabeth and a powerful statement of faith: "For with God nothing will be impossible" (Luke 1:37 NKJV).

God is the only one who inhabits the vast realm of impossibility. Every other created thing has limits. But through His Son, God has given Himself to us as an inheritance. Now, by our faith in Him, we have access to that very same heavenly reality where nothing is impossible (see Matthew 17:20).

God has given us access to Himself and has invited us into a union with Him to see all darkness bow to Him. Because nothing is impossible with God, and because we are called to co-labor with Him, we are required to take risks.

Children raised with this powerful Kingdom mindset will be able to look at any problem—in their personal lives, their city, their nation or the world—and know that God has a solution. Not only that, but they will know that the One with all the solutions lives inside them.

God wants to use His kids to bring His *shalom*—the wholeness and harmony of heaven—to the earth. Knowing this, it is our job to step out in faith in the face of poverty, brokenness, disease or pain and take the risks necessary to see heaven invade every situation for the glory of God. And it is our job to teach our children to do the same.

There is no limit to what our children can do when they live submitted to the Spirit of God. The same Holy Spirit who raised Christ from the dead lives in us and in our children, flowing through us to alter the course of history for His name's sake.

Jesus said to him, "If you can believe, all things are possible to him who believes." *Mark 9:23 NKJV*

Jesus looked at them and said, "With man this is impossible, but with God all things are possible." *Matthew 19:26 NIV*

O Sovereign LORD! You made the heavens and earth by your strong hand and powerful arm. Nothing is too hard for you! *Jeremiah 32:17 NLT*

I am so grateful, God, that in our own strength we don't have to do the things You have called us to do. Lord, help me build in ___ an awareness of Your heart to restore the world to Yourself, as well as Your empowerment to use ___ to invade every impossible situation. Holy Spirit, give me the wisdom to know how to build ___'s faith as we encounter situations that cry out for an invasion of Your Kingdom.

FOR TIME WITH
Your CHILD

ASK: What would you try to change about the world if you knew that you would be successful?

PRAY: *God, help me see that nothing is impossible with You. I know that You can do anything, but I want to understand in my heart that I can do anything when I'm doing it with You.*

DECLARE: With God, nothing is impossible for me!

DO: Decide on one area of "impossibility" in your family, your city or the world and pray together for God's power to invade that area.

5

Jesus' Blood Paid for Everything

Everything we will ever need was dealt with at the cross. The blood of Jesus purchased it all. Without the weight of sin dividing us, we are free to enter fully into the love and grace of the Father. Ephesians says that "in the ages to come He might show the exceeding riches of His grace in His kindness toward us in Christ Jesus" (Ephesians 2:7 NKJV). A hundred billion years from now, we will just be scratching the surface of understanding His grace.

The blood of Jesus purchased for you and for us all everything we will need throughout eternity, for every responsibility we face in life. We can face each challenge with confidence because we are not fighting *for* victory, but *from* victory. We are fighting *from* the triumph of Christ *toward* the situations that every one of us faces. The sacrifice of Jesus wiped out the debt of sin and restored us in our relationship with God's perfect love, protection and provision.

Because Jesus paid the price that took care of everything we owed, we owe Him our trust when things do not look like what we were expecting. Because His blood paid for everything, we don't need to worry. His grace has gone before us.

This is a powerful lesson for our children and grandchildren to begin learning in the home. There will be many times in their lives when things don't turn out exactly as they had imagined. But worry is just trust in the wrong god. When we can choose to trust God instead of remaining in fear or disappointment, and when we anchor ourselves in Him instead of in our circumstances, we build a foundation of faith within our lives.

God has already provided everything we will ever need. And from that place of assurance, we can boldly claim all that was purchased at Calvary. We can teach our children that bold faith stands on the shoulders of quiet trust.

For **MEDITATION**

He is so rich in kindness and grace that he purchased our freedom with the blood of his Son and forgave our sins. *Ephesians 1:7 NLT*

For my body is real food for your spirit and my blood is real drink. The one who eats my body and drinks my blood lives in me and I live in him. The Father of life sent me, and he is my life. In the same way, the one who feeds upon me, I will become his life. *John 6:55–57*

For God was pleased to have all his fullness dwell in him, and through him to reconcile to himself all things, whether things on earth or things in heaven, by making peace through his blood, shed on the cross. *Colossians 1:19–20 NIV*

Thank You for Your unending kindness, mercy and grace, Jesus. You sacrificed Yourself so that we could participate in Your eternal life. I plead the blood of Jesus over ___ right now. I declare that ___ is covered by Your protection, enveloped in Your love, a recipient of Your overflowing blessings and free from any bondage of sin. I pray that ___ will experience the peace-filled righteousness found in living a life completely trusting in You, God. Thank You that I can trust You with ___'s life and destiny. Thank You that You love this child more than I ever could.

FOR TIME WITH
Your CHILD

ASK: Tell me about a time when things did not turn out the way you were expecting. Can you think of one way that Jesus showed you His love in that moment? If not, ask Him to show you how He did!

PRAY: *Jesus, thank You for everything You did on the cross for me. Thank You for loving me so much that You would die for me. Help me become more and more like You every day.*

DECLARE: I can trust in Jesus no matter what! On the cross, He took care of everything I will ever need.

DO: Make a list of three to five declarations that you and/or your child can make the next time things are not going as planned. Keep these on hand so you can declare them together.

6

Born with Significance

Jesus tells us the commandment that is second most important, after loving God Himself, is to "love your neighbor as yourself" (Mark 12:31 NKJV). We know that loving others is important to do, but sometimes it is easy to forget that the standard by which we are able to love others is set by how much we understand our own value. We cannot give away a higher level of love than we are able to receive.

God calls us royalty (see 1 Peter 2:9). Jesus calls us friends and coheirs (see Hebrews 2:11). Our value is not defined by what we think about ourselves, but by who God says we are. We cannot afford to have a thought in our head about ourselves that He does not have in His.

God designed each person with a unique destiny and significance for this specific time on the earth. Your presence on the earth, the timing of your children or grandchildren's births—none of these were an accident. God designed your descendants with personalities He has known intimately since before the creation of the world. As the adults in these children's lives, we get to remind them of this daily. Once they know who God made them to be, they will never want to be anyone else.

Understanding their significance is never meant to become a source of entitlement or selfishness in our children. Jesus knew that the Father had given Him all authority in heaven and on the earth. He knew He was divine royalty—the Son of God—and from that awareness of His identity, Jesus washed His disciples' feet. He then told them, "If I then, your Lord and Teacher, have washed your feet, you also ought to wash one another's feet. For I have given you an example, that you should do as I have done to you" (John 13:14–15 NKJV). Because we know our significance, we can serve others well.

Are not two sparrows sold for a penny? Yet not one of them will fall to the ground outside your Father's care. And even the very hairs of your head are all numbered. So don't be afraid; you are worth more than many sparrows. *Matthew 10:29–31 NIV*

How thoroughly you know me, Lord! You even formed every bone in my body when you created me in the secret place, carefully, skillfully shaping me from nothing to something. You saw who you created me to be before I became me!

Psalm 139:14–16

Long before he laid down earth's foundations, he had us in mind, had settled on us as the focus of his love, to be made whole and holy by his love.

Ephesians 1:4 MESSAGE

God, You knit identity and value into every cell of ___'s body, mind and spirit. Father, I ask You to show me ways to encourage ___ and speak life into who You created this child to be. Show me ways to express how precious ___ is to You and to me. Thank You that You are our source of love. Help me be a better recipient of Your tender love so I can pour out even more of Your affection onto those around me, including onto ___. Holy Spirit, help me slow down and really see this amazing little person in front of me—one with a destiny given by God Himself. Show me opportunities to serve the people around me, Lord, modeling for ___ what servant-hearted leadership looks like.

FOR TIME WITH
Your CHILD

ASK: What do you think are some of the special ingredients God used to make you who you are? Tell me some of the great things about yourself.

PRAY: *Thank You, God, that You made me on purpose, with a special destiny for my life. Help me show the other people around me how important they are as well.*

DECLARE: I am important. How God made me is amazing!

DO: Think of one person you can honor today. Make a card together, make a phone call or tell the person face-to-face why you think he or she is so special.

7

Supernatural Kids

We want to protect our kids from many different things, especially in their young and tender years. Setting boundaries and guarding our children is an important part of intentional parenting. But the flip side is also true. We want to be intentional about exposing the children in our care to positive things.

One of the most valuable things we can do is expose our children to the things of God—to His Word, His nature and His supernatural power. Children need to see examples of the intimate involvement of God in their lives and in the lives of those around them.

Joshua 24:31 reads, "Israel served the Lord all the days of Joshua and all the days of the elders who survived Joshua, and had known all the deeds of the Lord which He had done for Israel" (NASB). Joshua was a spiritual father to a nation, and it was his exposure to the mighty deeds of God that empowered him as a leader.

Yet Joshua would not have learned a specific leadership ability by seeing manna appear on the ground every day. There probably was not a direct correlation for him between water springing from a rock and having the necessary skills to lead a nation. What Joshua did have, however, was an acute awareness that God was with him. He could see the unseen possibility in any situation. This changed his entire perspective on reality (see Numbers 13–14). He trusted God in all things, and it was this integral part of his history that made him a great leader.

While it is important for each of us to see the works of God for ourselves so we can teach and influence our children, it is exponentially more powerful to have our children see God's works for themselves. It is worth whatever the cost in time, money and risk to expose our children to miracles, signs and wonders, supernatural healings and the tangible nature of God's presence. The power of God will leave a permanent mark of God on them.

Come and see the works of God, who is awesome in His deeds toward the sons of men. *Psalm 66:5 NASB*

We've heard true stories from our fathers about our rich heritage. We will continue to tell our children and not hide from the rising generation the great marvels of our God—his miracles and power that have brought us all this far. *Psalm 78:3–4*

Your eyes have seen every great act of the LORD which He did.

Therefore you shall keep every commandment which I command you today, that you may be strong, and go in and possess the land which you cross over to possess. *Deuteronomy 11:7–8 NKJV*

You have filled the earth with evidence of Your supernatural power, God. Help me open my eyes to see where You are moving so that I can expose ___ to moments of Your divine intervention. Help me step over the boundary of inconvenience, fear of disappointment or my own discomfort so that ___ can begin to build a history of miracles with You right now. Thank You for all the ways Your love has brought breakthrough into my life. I promise to share the stories of Your goodness with ___, building an awareness of who You are and an expectation that this child will see Your hand move miraculously in the world.

ASK: Have you ever seen a miracle for yourself? If you have not seen one yet, what is one miracle that you would really love to see with your own eyes?

PRAY: *God, thank You that You are still doing miracles today. I pray for opportunities to see Your supernatural power invade the world around me.*

DECLARE: Our God is a miracle-working God! I am seated in heavenly places with Jesus, and nothing is too big or too broken for Him.

DO: Think of one person you know who needs a miracle, and pray together for that person.

I will pour water
on him who is thirsty,
and floods on the dry
ground; I will pour
My Spirit on your
descendants, and
My blessing on your
offspring.

ISAIAH 44:3 NKJV

8

Hearing God's Voice

God loves to speak to His children. In Jeremiah 33:3, He promises that He will not be silent: "Call to Me and I will answer you, and I will tell you great and mighty things, which you do not know" (NASB). There is no age requirement on learning to hear His voice. In fact, the earlier we start creating an environment where our children expect to hear from the Lord, the more natural it will be for them.

Yet any age is a good age to learn to hear God's voice. Hearing Him does not need to be spooky, somber or even particularly challenging. Every child was designed to hear the Creator's voice.

As parents and caregivers, we can make it simple and fun to learn to hear God. We can start by sharing our everyday experiences hearing His voice. Did you have an impression when you were talking to someone? Did you feel peace in a certain place? Did a specific Bible verse jump out at you? Tell your children or grandchildren!

We can let the children in our lives see by example that God speaks in many different ways. If an impression leads us to pray for someone, to release a healing miracle or to give a prophetic word, we can include our children in the process. When children see how hearing God's voice can impact others in miraculous ways, it creates within them both an expectation and an increased appetite for hearing Him for themselves.

As our kids' expectation to hear God grows, we can invite them to participate in simple decisions. Until they have their own history with God, however, asking them what God said to them can make them feel as if they are under pressure. Instead, we can ask something like, "What do you think God would be saying in this situation?" This keeps the stakes lower and helps children develop their gift of hearing.

If we believe God can use children, we must make room for their involvement in our efforts to love and minister to people. Learning to empower kids (within our guidance) is vital in order for them to become all God designed them to be—giant-killers who shape the course of world history.

For MEDITATION

My sheep hear My voice, and I know them, and they follow Me. *John 10:27 NKJV*

When the Spirit of truth comes, he will guide you into all truth. He will not speak on his own but will tell you what he has heard. He will tell you about the future. *John 16:13 NLT*

I hear the Lord saying, "I will stay close to you, instructing and guiding you along the pathway for your life. I will advise you along the way and lead you forth with my eyes as your guide." *Psalm 32:8*

Thank You, God, that You long to speak to ___. You have created ___ to be able to hear Your voice, and You want to talk to ___ even more than this child wants to hear from You. You have given ___ Your Holy Spirit, who leads us in Your ways and reveals the truth about every situation. You are with us all the time, and You will instruct and guide ___ every step of the way. Thank You that You want to share Your heart, sharing great and mighty things with ___ about the present and the future.

ASK: If you could imagine the most peaceful place to go and hang out with Jesus, what would it be like? What would you do together? What do you think Jesus would say to you?

PRAY: *Thank You, God, that You like talking to me. Help me learn all the special ways that You love to share things with me.*

DECLARE: Hearing God's voice is easy! He is speaking to me all the time.

DO: Think of one of your friends or neighbors. What do you think God would want to say to that person if He were standing in front of him or her right now? What do you think God loves about that person?

9

Born for War

We were born into a war. This is true of everyone, including our children. We don't want to live overly conscious of what the enemy is trying to do in the world, but it is helpful to be aware of how the devil can show up. He came to steal, kill and destroy. If we see any aspect of destruction, we can be confident that he is at work.

Jesus came, however, to bring abundant life (see John 10:10). Our children can begin to understand this difference so that they can pick up on when the enemy is trying to trick them into thinking the way he does. So often, the battle is for our minds.

Children can be particularly sensitive to the spiritual atmosphere, so it is important to give them the tools to empower them in any situation. We need to teach them about four powerful weapons they can use to meet challenges like nightmares, fear or anxiety, or even seeing things in the spirit that are not from God. These four weapons are the blood of Jesus, God's Word, the name of Jesus and praise.

The blood of Jesus sets us free. Because of His blood, we have the legal right to every victory in Christ for all eternity. Pleading the blood of Jesus over our lives emphasizes by faith the reality that already exists for us.

The Word of God is a most powerful weapon. It is by the Word of the Lord that creation was made. And it is by the Word of the Lord that we are equipped to fight.

The name of Jesus is a tower of strength, a hiding place in battle (see Proverbs 18:10). The devil fears the name of Jesus, and he fears us as we function in Jesus' name.

Finally, praise is powerful. When we lift God high in praise, His enemies are scattered (see Psalm 68:1–2). Praise is God focused, not devil focused, and God is the one who makes praise powerful against the powers of darkness. Keeping our eyes fixed on Him is our most effective weapon.

For MEDITATION

Submit yourselves, then, to God. Resist the devil, and he will flee from you. *James 4:7 NIV*

Put on the full armor of God, so that you will be able to stand firm against the schemes of the devil. For our struggle is not against flesh and blood, but against the rulers, against the powers, against the world forces of this darkness, against the spiritual forces of wickedness in the heavenly places. *Ephesians 6:11–12 NASB*

For although we live in the natural realm, we don't wage a military campaign employing human weapons, using manipulation to achieve our aims. Instead, our spiritual weapons are energized with divine power to effectively dismantle the defenses behind which people hide. We can demolish every deceptive fantasy that opposes God and break through every arrogant attitude that is raised up in defiance of the true knowledge of God. We capture, like prisoners of war, every thought and insist that it bow in obedience to the Anointed One. *2 Corinthians 10:3–5*

Thank You, Jesus, that Your death and resurrection mean that we are victorious over all the powers of darkness. I ask You to come near to ___ with Your presence. I pray that angels would stand guard over ___ by night and by day. Thank You that no fear, pain, sickness or torment is allowed to stay. Today, ___ and I put on the full armor of God, confident that You have demolished every deception and tool of the enemy. Thank You that You have invited us to stand victorious with You!

ASK: Have you ever had a scary thought come into your head, or had a nightmare while you slept? What weapons do you think God has given you to get those scary thoughts out of there?

PRAY: *Father, thank You that You have given my spirit such powerful armor. I am on the winning team, and I know that I can look to You anytime I feel scared.*

DECLARE: Jesus has made me strong and victorious. I am not afraid. All of heaven is on my side!

DO: Pick out a Bible verse and a worship song that you and/or your child can sing anytime you need a reminder that our all-powerful God is on your side.

10

Equipped for Victory

Any area of our lives in which we have no hope is under the influence of a lie. There is no situation we can face as parents or otherwise that God has not already prepared us for, and no situation for which He does not already have an answer.

When God freed the Israelites from Egypt and brought them out of captivity, their mindsets were still stuck in slavery. God therefore made the decision not to lead them by way of the land where the Philistines lived, even though it was a shorter route. He thought they might change their minds and go back to Egypt if they faced a war, so instead of leading them into battle at that time, He led them through the wilderness to the Red Sea (see Exodus 13:17–18).

With God on their side, the Israelites were fully capable of beating the enemy. But they did not yet trust in His faithful provision, so He redirected them. What does this tell us about the Lord? He will only lead us into battles He has already equipped us to win.

It is not sin to experience fear when we are facing a battle. But the offspring of fear is hopelessness, and we arrive in that place when we lose track of what God has already instilled in our lives. We all have some areas in life where we feel successful, and then other areas that are not working quite so well.

Our children experience the same thing. But together we can ask God to show us how He has equipped us for victory. We can lead our children into a time of remembering what they have seen, experienced or read in God's Word—things that have actually given them the tools for whatever situation they are facing. Our children are already equipped for victory.

"And everything I've taught you is so that the peace which is in me will be in you and will give you great confidence as you rest in me. For in this unbelieving world you will experience trouble and sorrows, but you must be courageous, for I have conquered the world!" *John 16:33*

You see, every child of God overcomes the world, for our faith is the victorious power that triumphs over the world. *1 John 5:4*

The LORD said to Joshua, "Do not be afraid of them; I have given them into your hand. Not one of them will be able to withstand you." *Joshua 10:8 NIV*

Father, thank You that I can rest in You with great confidence no matter what I'm facing. It is not a surprise to You that this world comes with difficult and heartbreaking circumstances, but You have conquered all of that! Holy Spirit, fill ___'s heart with Your courage. God, let ___ be increasingly aware that You have set us up for victory in every battle that we face. Help ___ replace all fear with a deep trust in You, knowing that You have been victorious already.

ASK: Is there a school subject, relationship or other area in your life that it feels hard to have hope about right now? What do you think God feels about that situation?

PRAY: *Thank You, God, that You care about every circumstance that feels hard to me. You never leave me alone in my battles. You go before me and set me up to win every time.*

DECLARE: God has set me up for victory in every battle!

DO: Take whatever battle is facing you and together ask the Lord what tools He has already given you so that you can be victorious.

11

Planting Seeds of Hunger

The Bible says of Samuel, "Now Samuel did not yet know the LORD, nor had the word of the LORD yet been revealed to him" (1 Samuel 3:7 NASB). As a young boy, Samuel ministered to the Lord not out of a personal relationship with Him, but because it was what he had been taught to do. In fact, it was not until the Lord called to him for the fourth time one night that his personal relationship with God began. Suddenly, all the training Samuel had received, all the moments he had spent in God's presence in practical service and worship, must have made sense to him.

As parents and grandparents, we don't want to create empty religious rituals for our children to follow, but we do have a pivotal role in training them in the ways of loving and worshiping God. We can teach them what personal devotion looks like, and in this way set them up with momentum in their relationship with God.

David raised his son Solomon with purpose and destiny in mind. In Proverbs 4:3–7, Solomon described the training he had received from his father, recalling some of David's words to him when he was a young boy: "Get wisdom! Get understanding!" (verse 5 NKJV).

David planted seeds of hunger for wisdom in his son, teaching him what to prioritize. This teaching was so ingrained in Solomon that when the Lord asked him to choose anything he wanted—even though Solomon was asleep at the time and was in the middle of a dream—he was able to say, "Give Your servant an understanding heart" (1 Kings 3:9 NASB).

As parents, we prepare our children with training that carries prophetic significance. Our instruction prepares them to make choices they may not have had access to make without the training for it. Perhaps Solomon is the only one in the Bible to whom God gave the *you can ask for anything you want* option because he was the only one prepared to make such a decision. David had trained him with destiny in mind.

We, too, get to plant seeds of hunger in our children by preparing them with destiny in mind. We do this through our prayer, teaching and encouragement. We then have the privilege of watching God respond to their readiness by giving them opportunities they may not have otherwise had as they step into their destinies.

Fathers, don't exasperate your children, but raise them up with loving discipline and counsel that brings the revelation of our Lord. *Ephesians 6:4*

Whatever you have learned or received or heard from me, or seen in me—put it into practice. And the God of peace will be with you. *Philippians 4:9 NIV*

So He humbled you, allowed you to hunger, and fed you with manna which you did not know nor did your fathers know, that He might make you know that man shall not live by bread alone; but man lives by every word that proceeds from the mouth of the LORD. *Deuteronomy 8:3 NKJV*

Father, help me teach ___ the ways of loving and worshiping You. Help me guide ___ without causing exasperation. I want ___ to be so familiar with Your ways, Holy Spirit, that an infrastructure of Your presence is built in Your child's heart. Help me lead ___ by example so that I can say with confidence, "Follow me, and the God of peace will be with you." Holy Spirit, help me see every opportunity for instructing ___ in the ways of God, so that all of heaven's opportunities would be poured out on this child.

ASK: What kinds of things do you think Samuel had to learn as a boy in order to minister to the Lord? What helps you when you are trying to learn something?

PRAY: *God, I want to learn and practice all the ways of loving and worshiping You.*

DECLARE: I am being trained to be a warrior for God!

DO: Think of some ways that together, you could pour out your love to God and worship Him.

12

Praying from His Presence

Prayer is a journey of joy. Much of the Church has a common misconception that intercession requires feeling heaviness and depression. It is as if intercessors have been told that they need to carry the weight of the world on their shoulders. But the reality is that Jesus already carried all the heaviness to the cross. We now get to carry joy in intercession because of who God is.

Intercession is birthed from a place of intimacy. God is calling us into a relationship with Him, showing us how He moves and works in various situations. There are times for travail or grieving, but if we leave our times of prayer and communion with Him unhappy, we have missed an opportunity to see what He is doing.

Whenever our worship gets replaced by worry, or whenever our prayers sound more like complaining, it is a clue that our thought life has become anchored in an inferior reality. But when we are able to move back into the place of absolute surrender, giving thanks and celebrating God's faithfulness in the midst of a situation we would like to see changed, we are winning the battle over our minds. We are stepping back into a place of intimacy with the Father and seeing the world as He sees it.

Such intimacy comes from time spent with Him. Hours spent in His presence are a precious thing, but there are seasons to our prayer life. If you are the parent of young children, for example, hours spent exclusively with God may not often be possible. That's fine. Instead, turn your heart toward Him in affection as you wash the dishes. Worship Him in the car as you drive your kids to school. Invite the Holy Spirit to increase your awareness of Him throughout your day.

Rather than striving to pray, we can invest in connecting with God's presence. That way, we become more aware of God's heart for different situations, and because of that, our prayer life becomes intentional and effective. The strength of our prayer is actually determined by the place from which we pray.

For MEDITATION

Be anxious for nothing, but in everything by prayer and supplication, with thanksgiving, let your requests be made known to God; and the peace of God, which surpasses all understanding, will guard your hearts and minds through Christ Jesus. *Philippians 4:6–7 NKJV*

Then you will call on me and come and pray to me, and I will listen to you. *Jeremiah 29:12 NIV*

So now we come freely and boldly to where love is enthroned, to receive mercy's kiss and discover the grace we urgently need to strengthen us in our time of weakness. *Hebrews 4:16*

Thank You, Lord, that Your Word promises that when I pray with thanksgiving and submit myself fully to Your hands, Your peace will be my protection. Father, I long to pray effective prayers that are anchored in Your presence and Your will for the earth. Help me teach ___ to come boldly before You to receive Your love, the strength of Your mercy and Your tender affection. Thank You that ___ can call on You as a child of God, and that You have promised to listen.

FOR TIME WITH
Your CHILD

ASK: What do you like to talk to God about? How do you feel after you talk to Him?

PRAY: *Thank You that I can talk to You about anything, Jesus. You always listen to me, so I can bring any worry to You and exchange it for Your peace.*

DECLARE: I know that God hears my prayers! His answers are always best for me.

DO: Spend a few minutes turning your affection toward God together. If you like, put on some gentle worship music, close your eyes and imagine His presence close to you. After that, share anything you experienced during that time and pray for one another.

13

Dreaming with God

God tells us that He did not choose a city in which to build His temple. It was David's dream to build God's temple, and God had chosen David (see 1 Kings 8:16). David's dreams were celebrated because they arose from his intimate relationship with the Lord.

What we give influence to in our lives shapes our desires. Although this is not a linguistic breakdown, even the word *desire—de* meaning "of" and *sire* meaning "of the father"—illustrates that our dreams and desires flow from that which we allow to have an impact on us. Our focus should be less on worrying whether or not our dreams come directly from God, and more on keeping our eyes locked on the things of heaven.

The offspring of our heart is desire. If we spend most of our time, for example, contemplating the things we lack and how to get them, our desires will reflect and be limited by this self-centered mindset. But as we walk with the Lord, learning to become tender and sensitive to His presence, dreams begin to form within us that reflect the environment of heaven.

The Church has not always encouraged believers to enjoy the freedom to express the resurrected life of Christ through their dreams and desires. We have said yes to discipleship, obedience and servanthood—all of which are important—but we have not always known what it looks like to be a friend of God. Friends steward relationships differently than servants. A servant keeps a checklist of accomplished tasks, but friends of God are concerned with how their actions and dreams impact His heart.

The Lord created each of us with specific passions and strengths for a reason. The world is crying out for God's Kingdom to be revealed (see Romans 8:19). God wants each person fully revealed as His son or daughter. He has placed dreams into our hearts and the hearts of our children and grandchildren that will illustrate Him in a way that meets the cry of an orphaned planet.

God longs for people who are free to think for themselves—not independently of Him, but because of their intimate relationship with Him. Our role is to encourage our children and grandchildren to dream with God, planting words of hope and promise into the world around them.

May He grant you according to your heart's desire, and fulfill all your purpose. *Psalm 20:4 NKJV*

We have become his poetry, a re-created people that will fulfill the destiny he has given each of us, for we are joined to Jesus, the Anointed One. Even before we were born, God planned in advance our destiny and the good works we would do to fulfill it! *Ephesians 2:10*

Let the words of my mouth and the meditation of my heart be acceptable and pleasing in Your sight, O LORD, my [firm, immovable] rock and my Redeemer. *Psalm 19:14 AMP*

Lord, thank You that You are the one who has placed dreams within my heart. Thank You that as I spend time with You, the atmosphere of Your presence births desires in me that will impact the world for Your glory. Help me reflect that kind of empowerment to ___ as the dreams and visions You have placed in this child's heart begin to emerge. Holy Spirit, give me the wisdom not to squash ___'s dreams, even if they seem scary to me. Thank You that ___ will be part of a generation that knows You are the God of the impossible. Thank You that You have given ___ a destiny to fulfill, and that ___'s dreams are good.

FOR TIME WITH
Your CHILD

ASK: What does your dream life, meaning the things you desire, look like? If you could dream up a way to help people, what would it be?

PRAY: *God, thank You that You care about the dreams of my heart. Help me dream with confidence, knowing You are on my side.*

DECLARE: God cares about my dreams. I can boldly share them with Him!

DO: Without prioritizing them, create a list of ten dreams together. These dreams can be anything you can think of or imagine! Read them out loud to one another.

14

Designed for Worship

The Bible says that the Lord is looking for worshipers; it does not say He is looking for worship (see John 4:23). Worship is our supreme responsibility. It is what we were created for. Being those who minister to the Lord in worship is the greatest call on our lives. It is not merely the songs we sing; it is the heartfelt honor we give God.

Everyone worships. The only question is who or what we are worshiping. Some people worship family, money, careers or even themselves. But the Lord in His mercy designed it so that we would find our fullest expression in life when we stand before Him—accepted and delighted in by our God—and ministering to Him with thanksgiving, praise and worship.

Worship is an intimate moment between God and us. But corporate church gatherings are also important for families. Even when children are very young and don't seem to be paying attention, there is value in honoring corporate times of worship. Children pick up spiritual things quite easily, even when they are playing with toys or drawing. Part of valuing church attendance is instilling within our children and grandchildren the discipline of doing the right thing even if they don't feel like it. Most of all, prioritizing corporate worship helps construct in them an internal value system where their "inner spirit" becomes trained.

Every thought and plan God has ever had for us has always been motivated completely by love. In His love, He chose to design us as worshipers. We always become like whatever we worship, and there is nothing better for us than to become like our Father. There is also no greater goal or plan than for us to be conformed into the image of His Son, Jesus.

As we pursue God, we become like Him (see 1 John 3:2). We are transformed according to our time in and exposure to the glory that is the manifest presence of King Jesus. Every time we take a moment to turn the affection of our heart toward the Lord, we are changed.

Let everyone everywhere join in the crescendo of ecstatic praise to Yahweh! Hallelujah! Praise the Lord! *Psalm 150:6*

Bless and affectionately praise the LORD, O my soul, and all that is [deep] within me, bless His holy name. *Psalm 103:1 AMP*

From here on, worshiping the Father will not be a matter of the right place but with the right heart. For God is a Spirit, and he longs to have sincere worshipers who worship and adore him in the realm of the Spirit and in truth. *John 4:23–24*

I worship You, God! I honor who You are in my life, in my family's lives and in the world. You are so worthy of my praise! Lord, let my adoration of You spill over and impact my family. I declare that ___ will also be a mighty worshiper. This child will overflow with deep affection for Your presence. ___'s life will reveal a heart laid down in worship of Your holy name. Holy Spirit, I value Your presence in my life above all else. Help me keep my identity as a worshiper in the forefront of my mind at all times, and help ___ to do the same.

ASK: In what ways do you like to worship God? How do you think He feels when you worship Him?

PRAY: *God, You are so easy to love and give praise to! Thank You that I get to spend my whole life adoring You.*

DECLARE: I am a worshiper for life!

DO: Think of a fun new way to worship the Lord together. Maybe it is through dancing, singing, painting or resting quietly in His presence.

15

Trust in Him

The secret things belong to the LORD our God" (Deuteronomy 29:29 NASB). We all have questions about various areas of life, particularly in parenting. Yet this verse implies that we are required to trust God before we understand why, how or what to do. The realm of mystery is as important in our lives as the realm of revelation. The more we trust God with things we cannot understand, the more He trusts us with that which we can understand.

When we come face-to-face with something we cannot explain, it both challenges our faith and reveals it. Jesus tells us that God has given us the "mysteries of the kingdom of heaven" as our inheritance (Matthew 13:11 NASB). So we live within this tension: The mysteries of the Kingdom are within our reach, but they are not all within our possession. And trust is what we do—how we position our hearts—in the in-between.

Many people trust God easily, until a problem arises. Then their confusion can turn into accusation: *God, I thought You said . . .* But He is incredibly patient. He invites us to come to Him in prayer, with honesty, but we do not have the right to understand everything unless He reveals it to us. God is trying to cultivate within us a quiet foundation of trust that He can then build upon.

It is in the act of believing that Jesus is the Son of God that we are born again (see John 1:12). The Lord is working to bring us into absolute confidence in who He is. Trust is not merely a mental agreement, a concept or a doctrine. It is casting the weight of our lives into a place of complete abandonment to who He is. We can only receive Him to the measure that we trust Him. Receiving Him is what gives us the authority to become mirrors of His nature—sons and daughters of God—carrying the actual nature of Christ into the earth.

May everyone who knows your mercy keep putting their trust in you, for they can count on you for help no matter what. O Lord, you will never, no never, neglect those who come to you. *Psalm 9:10*

You will keep in perfect and constant peace the one whose mind is steadfast [that is, committed and focused on You—in both inclination and character], because he trusts and takes refuge in You [with hope and confident expectation].

Isaiah 26:3 AMP

But blessed are those who trust in the LORD and have made the LORD their hope and confidence.

Jeremiah 17:7 NLT

I am intimately acquainted with Your mercy, God, so I will put my trust in You every day. I give up my right to understand everything You are doing in my life. I release my life and the lives of my family members, including ___, back into Your capable hands. Thank You that ___ will always be able to count on Your help. You will never neglect ___. Holy Spirit, help me keep my mind focused on who God is, that my entire household would be kept in His perfect and constant peace. You are our hope and confidence, Lord. I trust You completely.

ASK: What do you think it looks like for God to be holding the whole world in His hands?

PRAY: *Thank You, God, that I can put all my trust in You. Even when I don't understand something, You do understand it, so I don't need to worry.*

DECLARE: You are faithful. I trust You, God, no matter what!

DO: On a piece of paper, express one area of your life that you want to place in God's trustworthy hands. You can write it down, or you can get as creative as you want—coloring, drawing, making a collage! Then hang the paper somewhere that you can see it as a reminder to trust God.

They shall be My people, and I will be their God; and I will give them one heart and one way, that they may fear Me always, for their own good and for the good of their children after them.

JEREMIAH 32:38–39 NASB

16

Choosing Joy

J oy is such an important heavenly commodity that it motivated Jesus to endure the pain and humiliation of the cross (see Hebrews 12:2). When God defined the nature of His Kingdom, He chose to describe it as righteousness, peace and joy (see Romans 14:17).

Joy, Scripture says, is a key to living in the strength of the Lord, and laughter is a key to health (see Nehemiah 8:10; Proverbs 17:22). Scripture also says that in the presence of God there "is fullness of joy" (Psalm 16:11 NASB). But it is important for both children and adults to realize that joy is not a byproduct of circumstances. It is a heart posture that God commands us to inhabit.

God tells the barren woman to rejoice before she has a child in her arms, and to celebrate wildly before the breakthrough: "Sing, barren woman . . . burst into song, shout for joy, you who were never in labor" (Isaiah 54:1 NIV). Each of us has some areas of fruitfulness and other areas of barrenness in our life. God tells us to face the thing where we have seen the least breakthrough—whether it is the salvation of a family member, a health condition, a parenting struggle or financial insecurity—and to display a deliberate, extreme expression of joy.

The barren woman's shout is one of anticipation, and ours should be, too. This is the discipline of joy. It is actually within our ability to choose joy. If it were not within the reach of our will, God would be cruel to command it. Joy ahead of time is an expression of our faith. It models for our children and grandchildren the ability to give thanks in the midst of all things, because it anticipates the goodness of God.

This joyful expression is unreasonable from a human perspective, but it is totally logical from God's perspective. It is the logical response when you lock eyes with the Promise Keeper, the one who has never lied, the one who is no respecter of persons, the one who is the same yesterday, today and forever. When our focus is on Him, anticipating His faithfulness with joy is the perfectly intelligent thing to do.

Go ahead and celebrate! Come on and clap your hands, everyone! Shout to God with the raucous sounds of joy! *Psalm 47:1*

Now may the God of hope fill you with all joy and peace in believing, so that you will abound in hope by the power of the Holy Spirit. *Romans 15:13 NASB*

Shout aloud and sing for joy, people of Zion, for great is the Holy One of Israel among you.

Isaiah 12:6 NIV

God, give me the faith of the barren woman who burst into song because she knew that her God was faithful. You are the fulfiller of promises, so I can choose to celebrate joyfully in anticipation of every breakthrough. Jesus, help me show ___ what it looks like to live in joyful anticipation of Your goodness. Fill ___ with Your hope, joy and peace every moment of the day.

FOR TIME WITH
Your CHILD

ASK: What does someone look like when he or she is filled with joy? Without using words, let's show each other what joy looks like!

PRAY: *Thank You, God, that You look after every area of my heart. Thank You that You are a good Father and that You want me to live with joy every day.*

DECLARE: God is faithful. Joy is important. I can celebrate every day, because He's got this!

DO: Put on your favorite song and have a dance party! Imagine that you are dancing on the places in your life where you want to see an answer to prayer.

17

Great Courage

There was a moment in Israel's history when one soldier, Jonathan, and his armor-bearer stood before an entire Philistine army. Jonathan turned to his servant and, in so many words, said, "I think we can take them" (see 1 Samuel 14:6). Against all effective military strategy, they crawled uphill on their hands and knees to meet the awaiting enemy. Yet when they got to the top of the hill, the entire army fell before them.

These two men illustrated such extraordinary valor that the report of their victory spread like wildfire through both Israel's camp and the Philistines' camp. In fact, the whole earth shook under the influence of their supernatural courage (see 1 Samuel 14:15). That day, the Israelites struck down the Philistines.

Our courage draws people out of complacency and into their destiny. Our courage prophesies to people, calling them out of hiding and back to their identity on the front lines of the battle.

One of the greatest enemies of living a life of great courage is the fear of man. Allowed an audience, the fear of man can masquerade as many other things—wisdom, an understanding heart, discernment—but it is actually a counterfeit for the fear of God. The fear of man will cripple us if we allow it to, forcing us to consider other people's opinions before we obey God. We are meant to fear only Him. If we don't live by the praises of others, we won't die by their criticisms.

As parents and grandparents, we are called to live a lifestyle of courage that honors God. We can draw from every biblical example we can find, refusing to let the size of the giants we face impress us. They are not worthy of the attention. God has already gone before us and set the stage for our triumph through the promises He has given us.

Live with that confidence in all of life. And let that confidence infuse your relationship with your children and grandchildren. God designed them to carry courage into all the earth. They were born for this.

For MEDITATION

Be on guard; stand firm in your faith [in God, respecting His precepts and keeping your doctrine sound]. Act like [mature] men and be courageous; be strong. Let everything you do be done in love [motivated and inspired by God's love for us].

1 Corinthians 16:13–14 AMP

———

"Have I not commanded you? Be strong and courageous. Do not be afraid; do not be discouraged, for the LORD your God will be with you wherever you go." *Joshua 1:9 NIV*

———

Lord, even when your path takes me through the valley of deepest darkness, fear will never conquer me, for you already have! You remain close to me and lead me through it all the way. Your authority is my strength and my peace. The comfort of your love takes away my fear. I'll never be lonely, for you are near. *Psalm 23:4*

Thank You, Lord, that You never leave me alone. Even when I am walking through the darkest seasons of my life, I can be filled with the confident courage that comes from knowing that You are right by my side. Holy Spirit, fill ___ with that same awareness. Open ___'s heart to Your love that takes away all fear. Help this child of Yours stand firm in faith, receiving Your strength and peace. Thank You, Jesus, that ___ and I never need to be afraid, for You are close to us, leading us through every situation.

ASK: Tell me about a moment when you felt really brave.

PRAY: *Jesus, fill my heart with Your courage. Thank You that even when I am feeling scared, I know I can trust in You. I never have to be afraid.*

DECLARE: I am brave and filled with courage! With God on my side, nothing else stands a chance!

DO: Talk together about a moment when you felt scared. Ask Jesus to fill you with His courage. Ask Him what His bravery looks like in that kind of situation.

18

A Grateful Heart

If there is one thing Beni and I would ask the Lord to impart to our children and grandchildren, it would be a thankful heart. Yet this is one aspect of spiritual maturity that none of us get through impartation; we get it through our own choices.

In the book of Nehemiah, people were assigned to give thanks to God as the wall around Jerusalem was rebuilt (see Nehemiah 12:27–47). This sounds formal and ritualistic to our ears, but there is a secret in the routine of choosing to give thanks. When we choose to give thanks, we bypass the limitations of our emotional condition by making mature choices that align our emotions with the call of God on our lives.

Forgetting to give thanks allows inferior circumstances to take the reins of our hearts, undermining our faith. Complaining happens when we are more mindful of a problem than we are of God. It is impossible to complain when we are more aware of the goodness of God than we are of any issue we face.

The Bible says to rejoice always (see 1 Thessalonians 5:16). No matter what happens, choose gratitude. Even when we don't feel like it, we are called to rejoice. That's why it is a choice. God would not command it if it were always going to feel natural. Because He has commanded it, however, we know that gratitude is always within our reach.

We also know that when our children learn to give thanks when things are difficult, it strengthens their character and "faith muscle." As we raise these precious young ones to carry the weightiness of God's glory into the earth, their ability to see beyond their emotional state becomes essential.

Gratitude gets easier the more aware we are that God has given us everything good in our lives (see James 1:17). This practice of being grateful aligns us with heaven, acknowledging God's hand in every area of our lives. Thankfulness takes what the enemy meant for evil and places it into the hands of our Father, who causes all things to work for His glory and our benefit (see Romans 8:28).

Therefore, since we are receiving a kingdom that cannot be shaken, let us be thankful, and so worship God acceptably with reverence and awe.

Hebrews 12:28 NIV

So let's keep on giving our thanks to God, for he is so good! His constant, tender love lasts forever!

Psalm 118:29

Rejoice always, pray without ceasing, in everything give thanks; for this is the will of God in Christ Jesus for you. *1 Thessalonians 5:16–18 NKJV*

Father, I am so grateful for who You are and for all You have done in my life. I want to fill my days with adoration and worship of You. You are so good. Thank You that ___ will witness me giving thanks in every situation, and that this child will know Your love is constant, tender and unchanging. Help ___ and me see the choice we have for expressing our gratitude in every moment. I long for both of us to be in constant communion with You, always aware of Your goodness.

FOR TIME WITH
Your CHILD

ASK: Tell me about an experience when someone did something for which you felt grateful. What are some ways you can show this person or someone else your gratitude?

PRAY: *Thank You, God, for everything You have done in my life. Help me remember that because of who You are, I can always be grateful no matter what is happening.*

DECLARE: I can be grateful no matter what. I have so many things to be thankful for!

DO: Taking turns, think of at least ten things for which you can thank God.

19

A Lifestyle of Forgiveness

There is always a reason for unforgiveness, and most children (and adults) are eager to defend their position when wronged. People can do horrible things to one another, but we are called to forgive others with the same forgiveness that Christ showed us.

If I carry unforgiveness, it does not hurt the person who hurt me; it defiles me and everyone who is under my influence. As someone once said, withholding forgiveness is like drinking poison and hoping the other person will die. It never really works.

Forgiving someone is never about that person's worth anyway, and we should be eternally grateful for that. There would be no more unforgiveness on our part if we could truly see how unworthy we were of forgiveness when Christ died for us. But forgiveness and trust are two different things. Just because you release someone from judgment does not mean you are required to trust that person in the same way as before. Trust has to be earned; forgiveness does not.

It is also okay to be angry. As parents, we are not meant to suppress our children's emotions. Anger at injustice is hardwired into our DNA, but anger must not develop into sin such as bitterness, self-promotion, resentment or retaliation. God has designed us to be those who enter into painful situations with a redemptive solution.

In Matthew 6:11–12 (NKJV), Jesus taught us how to begin each day in prayer: "Give us this day our daily bread. And forgive us our debts, as we forgive our debtors." So we begin our day by declaring our purpose to be people of redemption. Before others sin against us, we prepare ourselves to forgive. That way, our inner world won't be controlled by other people's actions.

The Bible also says not to let the sun go down on our anger (see Ephesians 4:26). So we end our day with forgiveness, releasing the pain of the day so that it does not take root and begin to define us.

Jesus did not call us to live a philosophy of forgiveness, but a lifestyle of releasing those around us from judgment as we submit in an act of obedience to the Father.

Tolerate the weaknesses of those in the family of faith, forgiving one another in the same way you have been graciously forgiven by Jesus Christ. If you find fault with someone, release this same gift of forgiveness to them. *Colossians 3:13*

For if you forgive others for their transgressions, your heavenly Father will also forgive you.

Matthew 6:14 NASB

Lay aside bitter words, temper tantrums, revenge, profanity, and insults. But instead be kind and affectionate toward one another. Has God graciously forgiven you? Then graciously forgive one another in the depths of Christ's love.

Ephesians 4:31–32

Thank You that You know us so well, God, that You have instructed us to bookend our days with the exercise of forgiveness. I could never have earned Your forgiveness, Lord. Help me remain aware of my dependence on Your grace and mercy, so that I can release others from judgment. Holy Spirit, also help me model forgiveness to ___. I want to be known as an easy forgiver, one who shows mercy to others and myself constantly. Help me ask ___ for forgiveness when I have done something wrong. Also help me restore ___ quickly and easily when this precious child makes a mistake.

ASK: Have you ever had a hard time forgiving someone? How did that feel?

PRAY: *Thank You, God, for forgiving me. Help me forgive others, even when they have really hurt me.*

DECLARE: God forgave me. He will always forgive me. So I can give forgiveness to others.

DO: Is there someone you need to forgive for something he or she did to you? Walk through forgiveness together and then think of a way to put that forgiveness into action.

20

Investing in Eternity

Generosity is an investment in eternity. As believers, we give to support the work of the ministry, to meet human need, and also because of who we are and whose we are. The Bible says Solomon gave gifts to the Queen of Sheba "according to the royal generosity" (1 Kings 10:13 NKJV). As a queen, she had no needs of her own, but Solomon gave her gifts as an expression of his royal identity.

As the Lord shifts our identity, our thinking changes. We stop asking, *Can we afford it?* Instead, our question becomes, *What is the Lord giving me the privilege to do?* Our generosity flows out from our identity as children of the King who has given us everything.

The Bible is clear that our tithe belongs to God, but the offerings we make above that can emerge from our passions. Whether we focus on social justice causes, education, missions or poverty, we get to sow into the places where our hearts burn to make a difference. And we get to include our children in the privilege of giving.

We can take practical steps toward developing in our children and grandchildren a value for giving. We can give them money for the sole purpose of giving it away. We can include them in giving to the person waiting outside the grocery store or to someone who needs help with food or gas. We get to stir up compassion in them, allowing them to experience the joy of generosity.

Paul says that when the church of Corinth gave, as a result he and others offered "thanksgiving to God" (2 Corinthians 9:11 NIV). We have the opportunity to act in a way that brings other people closer to God. To have that impact on others is stunning. Our generosity can shift someone's heart toward the Lord.

The Passion Translation actually says that an act of generosity toward an enemy will "awaken his conscience" (Proverbs 25:21–22). Through our radical generosity that reflects the abundance of heaven, we can turn hearts to the goodness of God, both honoring other people as masterpieces of His creation and awakening their spirits to an awareness of our good Father.

For MEDITATION

Give generously to them and do so without a
grudging heart; then because of this the LORD
your God will bless you in all your work and in
everything you put your hand to.

Deuteronomy 15:10 NIV

Let giving flow from your heart, not from a sense
of religious duty. Let it spring up freely from the
joy of giving—all because God loves hilarious
generosity! *2 Corinthians 9:7*

Instead, I've found the godly ones to be the generous ones who give freely to others. Their children
are blessed and become a blessing. *Psalm 37:26*

Jesus, You have given everything to us. You gave Your life, and because of Your unfathomable generosity, ___ and I get to inherit the Kingdom and everything in it. Holy Spirit, help me stay aware of all I have been given. I want to understand my identity so deeply that I can give freely from that place. Help me make generosity a pillar of our home, modeling that principle for ___ to see every day. I want to show ___ the joy of giving, so that this child will live a life of generosity, reaping the blessings that come from that mindset.

ASK: Tell me about a time when someone else was generous to you. How did that make you feel?

PRAY: *Jesus, thank You that You have been so generous with me. Help me live generously toward others. I want my generosity to show people how good You are.*

DECLARE: I am a child of the King. Because I know that, I am generous to everyone!

DO: Think of a person or family whom you could bless with generosity. Maybe it would mean leaving a note or cookies at their door, giving them money or cooking them a meal. Think of a way to show God's kindness to someone today!

21

Honor for Everyone

We are called to treat all people as Christ treats them. Every single person is made in the image of God and endowed with gifts and abilities from his or her Creator. Scripture tells us to fear the Lord (see Psalm 34:9). So if other people are Christians, we also get to have a healthy fear of and respect for Christ within them.

We can celebrate all that people are without stumbling over who they are not, because Christ did so for us. Jesus illustrated this with Peter, creating a culture of value for His disciples before they were able to earn it through their own strength. Peter's name was Simon, which meant "broken reed," but Jesus renamed him Peter, meaning "rock" (see Matthew 16:18). In the midst of Peter's brokenness and mistakes, Jesus called out this disciple's identity with honor.

In 1 Peter 2:13–15, Peter instructs us to submit ourselves to authority. He does not qualify this by saying that we should submit ourselves to good authority, or even that we should respect only

Christian authority. And he continues by saying, "Act as free men, and do not use your freedom as a covering for evil, but use it as bondslaves of God. Honor all people, love the brotherhood, fear God, honor the king" (verses 16–17 NASB). Our freedom is given to us not so that we can do what we want, but so that—freed from sin—we can follow Christ and do what is right.

In 1 Timothy 2:1–2, we are commanded to give thanks for all people. Expressing gratitude within your family, even for the most challenging members, sets the stage for honoring every single person as Christ does. This kind of unmitigated honor transforms not only the lives of individuals, but also the atmosphere of our homes and entire cities.

Paul continues by telling Timothy that when we blanket each person with gratitude and prayer, we usher in "peaceful and quiet lives in all godliness and holiness" (1 Timothy 2:2 NIV). When we bring a Christlike value for honor into our families, it infuses the atmosphere with the *shalom* of heaven, attracting others to the Kingdom of God (see 1 Timothy 2:3–4).

Be devoted to tenderly loving your fellow believers as members of one family. Try to outdo yourselves in respect and honor of one another. *Romans 12:10*

"Honor your father and mother." This is the first commandment with a promise: If you honor your father and mother, "things will go well for you, and you will have a long life on the earth." *Ephesians 6:2–3 NLT*

The Lord says:
"These people come near to me with their mouth and honor me with their lips, but their hearts are far from me. Their worship of me is based on merely human rules they have been taught." *Isaiah 29:13 NIV*

Forgive me, Father, for any dishonor of others I have modeled for ___. I want both of us to see each person the way You do, Jesus. Stir up our hearts toward thankfulness for each person who crosses our path. Help us honor You, God, with every word we speak and with every attitude of our heart. You have said that living with honor leads to a good, long life, and I want that for myself, for ___ and for my entire family. Holy Spirit, show me opportunities throughout the day when I can instill the value of honor into ___ and into my whole household.

ASK: What are some ways you can think of to honor the people around you?

PRAY: *Jesus, help me see other people the way You see them. Help me be grateful and give honor to everyone.*

DECLARE: Every person deserves my honor!

DO: Think of someone who feels a bit hard to be thankful for. What is one way you could show that person honor today?

22

Kingdom Authority

Government serves two major purposes, no matter what the institution or who its leader is—whether the president of a nation, the CEO of a corporation or the pastor of a church. Those two purposes are *to protect* and *to empower* the people under its authority.

The family is no different. God established the family as the bedrock of humanity, and parents are His governmental representatives who operate in the authority of heaven *to protect* and *to empower*—to defend and to equip—the children under their care.

For many people, the idea of authority can feel complicated. Often, people who have experienced unhealthy or abusive leadership can find themselves wanting to leave the whole concept of rulership behind. This is an understandable reaction to a wrong, but it is not what God calls us to do. He is zealous about the advancement of His Kingdom, and about us taking up the authority He has handed down to us through Jesus (see Isaiah 9:7; Matthew 28:18).

Yet alongside taking up our God-given authority, you and I are also called to become the servants of all (see Mark 9:35). We must learn, then, how to lead and how to serve. When we truly understand the Kingdom authority that we carry, we can rule with the heart of a servant, and serve with the heart of a king.

Ruling with the heart of a servant means that we lead with humility, making sure we use our authority for the benefit of others. Serving with the heart of a king means that we serve with confidence, knowing we must draw upon the unlimited resources of the King whom we serve. It is our expression of humility, combined with a backbone of confidence, that enables us to draw upon God's resources, as needed, to serve people effectively.

As parents and grandparents, we have an opportunity to represent the heart of God well in this area. We get to protect and to empower the children under our care, modeling noble service and servant-hearted leadership. God has made us tools in His hands—instruments shaping the values, character, gifts and thoughts of a generation. By reflecting God's heart within our positions of leadership, we uniquely position our children to represent God well in the earth as they take up positions of authority themselves one day.

Every person must submit to and support the authorities over him. For there can be no authority in the universe except by God's appointment, which means that every authority that exists has been instituted by God. So to resist authority is to resist the divine order of God, which results in severe consequences. *Romans 13:1–2*

Truly I tell you, whatever you bind on earth will be bound in heaven, and whatever you loose on earth will be loosed in heaven. *Matthew 18:18 NIV*

You make him to rule over the works of Your hands; You have put all things under his feet.

Psalm 8:6 NASB

God, You have placed authority over my life. Thank You for the chance I have to honor and respect the leaders You have instituted. Help me model that kind of support for ___, so that this child understands what healthy submission looks like. Holy Spirit, help me embody the qualities of Kingdom authority in my life and in my home. I want to be a source of protection and empowerment for ___. I want to lead with the heart of a servant and serve with the heart of a king so that ___ truly understands Your love, provision and protection. My heart is teachable and open to You, Holy Spirit. Give me the wisdom to implement authority with Your grace, mercy and truth.

FOR TIME WITH
Your CHILD

ASK: Tell me about one of the best teachers, coaches or church leaders you have had. What did you appreciate about that person?

PRAY: *Thank You, God, that I have people in authority in my family and in my life who love, protect and encourage me. Help me always honor the leaders You have given me.*

DECLARE: God has put authority over me for my benefit! I am safe and championed. I show the leaders in my life respect and honor.

DO: Together, think of one leader in your family, church or community whom you can honor for his or her leadership. Consider writing a note to that person (or to the person your child thought of in the "Ask" exercise).

23

The Context of Unity

God does not shy away from expressing His vision for marriage. He made it clear from the very beginning that the marriage covenant unites men and women in a mysterious way—causing them to leave their families and become one flesh (see Genesis 2:24).

Within that union, marriage points to the ultimate union of Jesus and His Bride, the Church. But it also gives us clear direction for the institution of family on the earth. The bond between husband and wife is sacred, yet God's intent for marriage does not stop there. "Didn't the LORD make you one with your wife? In body and spirit you are his. And what does he want? Godly children from your union" (Malachi 2:15 NLT).

God's intention is that from the union of man and wife, godly generations of children will be born. The purpose of marriage is to raise children who are prepared to step into their divine calling—becoming world-changers for His glory.

This does not exclude children from divided homes, of course. On the contrary, every family is entirely dependent on the grace of God to cover areas of weakness. Evidence is everywhere that God's grace is more than sufficient to make up for what is lacking in any household. God is clear, however, that the best option is for children to be raised in a unified home. From that context, they can most readily set forth with confidence to manifest God's nature and heart to the world.

God is gloriously revealed in the Gospel, but He is also made known through His creation, through art, through design and through people themselves. The list of ways He is revealed is endless. One of the clearest ways, however, is in the home—through how we live as a family. He is looking for a generation of giant-killers who will grow up in our homes to model and reflect His nature in all they say and do. This generation will demonstrate His perfect rule over all He has made, modeling "on earth as it is in heaven."

But Lord, your endless love stretches from one eternity to the other, unbroken and unrelenting toward those who fear you and those who bow facedown in awe before you. Your faithfulness to keep every gracious promise you've made passes from parents, to children, to grandchildren, and beyond. *Psalm 103:17*

Grandchildren are the crowning glory of the aged; parents are the pride of their children.

Proverbs 17:6 NLT

Therefore know that the LORD your God, He is God, the faithful God who keeps covenant and mercy for a thousand generations with those who love Him and keep His commandments.

Deuteronomy 7:9 NKJV

God, You value family so much. Thank You that You cover every deficit in our family with Your love and grace. Thank You that Your love stretches out over each one of our family members. Lord, You keep every promise You have made, and Your blessings will pass down to my lineage for a thousand generations. Holy Spirit, help me teach ___ to have Your value for unity within our family. Help me show ___ what it looks like to communicate bravely, to forgive easily and to fight for connection.

ASK: What is your favorite thing to do together as a family?

PRAY: *Thank You, Lord, that You love it when my family works together as a team. Thank You that You care about each and every one of us. Help us grow in our love and connection, showing the world what You look like.*

DECLARE: God loves my family! He is wrapping us all up together in His arms.

DO: Plan a fun activity you can do as a family. Whether it is eating a meal together, playing a game, watching a movie or going on an adventure, use this time to celebrate the connection and bonds in your family.

You are heirs of their prophecies and of the covenants God made with your fathers when he promised Abraham, "Your descendant will bring blessing to all the people on the earth."

ACTS 3:25

24

Creating a Testimony Culture

We are called to hold the record of God's miraculous interventions among His people—the testimonies—so closely that they become the lenses through which we see our present challenges. Revelation 19:10 says, "For the testimony of Jesus is the spirit of prophecy" (NASB). We therefore know that we can interpret our current circumstances through God's supernatural history. Instead of seeing a problem, we can see the opportunity for a miracle.

Psalm 78 exhorts us to train our children not only in the law and commandments of God, but also in the reports of His wonderful works. The Lord establishes a value system for the spoken and written records of His deeds that will be passed down to each generation. In verse 7 of this psalm, He tells us why: "That they may set their hope in God" (NKJV).

There is something about the testimony that positions our children and grandchildren to place their hope in God when a trial comes. Because they have been saturated by stories of God's supernatural intervention, their instinctive response can be, *I'm going to trust God. He's the God who works wonders. I don't know how He'll do it, but I trust Him.*

The testimony and the courage to obey God are connected. By stewarding the testimony, we set the stage for our children and grandchildren to obey God. Knowing that our God is faithful in impossible situations is the way our confidence in Him remains strong.

Sharing testimonies builds an awareness of the God who is with us and the God who is for us. Any family that makes testimonies a primary focus will experience great dividends. The very nature of these stories carries the revelation of God's heart and nature, which never change.

That means when we hear a story of what God has done for someone else, we are hearing a story of what He will do for us. He is no respecter of persons, and He is the same yesterday, today and forever (see Acts 10:34; Romans 2:11; Hebrews 13:8).

For MEDITATION

I will remember the deeds of the LORD; yes, I will remember your miracles of long ago. *Psalm 77:11 NIV*

I remember the days of old; I meditate on all Your works; I muse on the work of Your hands.

Psalm 143:5 NKJV

These commandments that I give you today are to be on your hearts. Impress them on your children. Talk about them when you sit at home and when you walk along the road, when you lie down and when you get up. *Deuteronomy 6:6–7 NIV*

Father, You have always been so good and so faithful to me. Thank You for giving us this tool of the testimonies to help us remember who You are and how much You love to show up in the lives of Your kids. Thank You that, whenever I am struggling to hear Your voice, I can always return to the testimonies of Your miraculous intervention in my life. Help me help ___ build a record of testimonies so that this child will always remember Your works. Holy Spirit, give me creative ideas to inspire ___ to record God's miracles and return to these stories often. Help me create a testimony culture in our family.

ASK: Tell me a story about a way that God showed up in your life, and I will tell you one of my favorite testimonies!

PRAY: *You have always been so good to me, Jesus. Thank You that whenever I remember the different ways that You have loved me, I can remind myself about who You are. Thank You that any story I read in the Bible about Your miraculous deeds counts as something You would do again!*

DECLARE: I am building a history of God's miracles in my life. What He has done in the past, He will do again!

DO: Together, write down on scraps of paper all the ways you have experienced God's goodness and miraculous intervention as a family this year. Place these examples in a jar on your counter and add to them whenever you can. This way, if you ever need encouragement as a family, you will have a record of testimonies to pull from anytime!

25

Loving God's Word

The Word of God is a wonderful gift from Him. It has been the target of wars and conflicts, with leaders of culture pronouncing its demise. And yet here it stands as the high standard for life, having been breathed by God Himself. It is our privilege to read it over and over again and to pass down a love for God's Word to future generations.

We all want our children and grandchildren to be successful. But it is very difficult to be successful eternally without a foundation in the Word of God. Other books are supplements for our walk with Christ, but our meal is the Scriptures. The Word of God is perfectly fit to speak into any and every situation in our lives and in the lives of our children.

We can encourage our children to begin building their own history with God in their Bibles. Find a translation your children can understand, and then encourage them to underline verses that stand out to them or mark the date to remember a moment when God spoke to them about a situation. Children won't always be able to explain what they have read in the Bible, but that's all right. God does not touch our minds first; He touches our hearts. And from there, understanding and transformation arise.

We all have some times when we are more hungry for the Word of God than usual. In the natural world, we get hungry from not eating, but in the Kingdom, we actually get hungry *by* eating. We want to put ourselves in a place where continual exposure to what God is saying actually creates an appetite for the Word itself. This is the discipline of reading the Scriptures.

We have an invitation to come and engage with God Himself as we read His Word that gives life. And He loves to set us up. We come to His Word faithfully, and our sovereign God sets us up for divine encounters that we need. The Word of God is our greatest treasure. It accurately reveals His will, His heart and His promise for our family and for us.

For MEDITATION

For the word of God is living and powerful, and sharper than any two-edged sword, piercing even to the division of soul and spirit, and of joints and marrow, and is a discerner of the thoughts and intents of the heart. *Hebrews 4:12 NKJV*

Truth's shining light guides me in my choices and decisions; the revelation of your word makes my pathway clear. *Psalm 119:105*

The grass withers and the flowers fall, but the word of our God endures forever. *Isaiah 40:8 NIV*

Thank You, God, for the gift of Your Word. Thank You that each verse is not merely good ideas bound together, but that it is Your living Word. Jesus, help me instill a value for the Scriptures in ___. Let ___ begin to build a history with Your Word, so that it can be a shining light that guides this child in all of life's decisions. Illuminate Your Word to my family, Lord. I invite Your Word to pierce my heart, cutting off anything that is not of You. Holy Spirit, help us implement practical ways to sow Your Word deep into our hearts.

ASK: What is your favorite story from the Bible? Why do you like it? What did it teach you?

PRAY: *Thank You that You love to talk to me through the pages of my Bible, God. Help me develop the habit of reading Your Word so I can encounter You there daily.*

DECLARE: I love the Bible! It is God's living Word. It has important things to say about my life.

DO: Choose a Bible verse that you would like to turn into a song. You can use a familiar tune, but trade out the original words for the Scriptures. Now sing it together!

26

Bound to Hope

Hope is the heartbeat of heaven. As such, it must become the heartbeat of our homes. God is not depressed, worried or fearful. When we are those things, it is apparent that His influence in us has diminished. He is God, and as God, He is in charge. We always have a reason to hope.

When we are hopeless, we have stepped outside our call and design. We have forgotten what God has said and promised. In these moments, we must confess and repent our way back to our proper position, until hope is restored. As we said earlier, any area of our life for which we have no hope is under the influence of a lie. Learning to recognize hopelessness enables us to address whatever would undermine our health and well-being as a family.

Zechariah 9:12 describes a people who are bound to hope: "Return to the stronghold, you prisoners of hope" (NKJV). The Bible's use of the word *hope* is different than our current cultural understanding. In the world, hope is often interchanged with the idea of wishing for something—a birthday present, no traffic, nice weather. But the biblical understanding of hope is the joyful anticipation of good. The term *stronghold* often refers to demonic activity, but in this verse it is quite the opposite. In this context, the stronghold of hope is a place of safety.

Anyone can have hope when the breakthrough has already come. What makes hope such a profound influence is that the biblical kind of hope is found in the midst of circumstances that don't look hopeful. The circumstances may deny the very promise God has given us for our lives, and yet in the middle of that situation we can joyfully anticipate a breakthrough.

We may not know whether a breakthrough will come this afternoon, tomorrow or next week. But by keeping our eyes trained on God, we know we have done our part. And we know that we serve a God who has a reputation for breaking into impossible situations and reversing their effects.

Such hope [in God's promises] never disappoints us, because God's love has been abundantly poured out within our hearts through the Holy Spirit who was given to us. *Romans 5:5 AMP*

The LORD takes pleasure in those who fear Him, in those who hope in His mercy. *Psalm 147:11 NKJV*

Therefore, with minds that are alert and fully sober, set your hope on the grace to be brought to you when Jesus Christ is revealed at his coming.

1 Peter 1:13 NIV

God, when my hope is placed in You instead of the circumstances around me, I will never be disappointed. Thank You that our hope in You brings You pleasure. Holy Spirit, remind me anytime I am feeling discouraged that our God is bigger than any problem I may be facing. Help my family and me banish hopelessness from our home. Give ___ eyes to see Your faithfulness, too, and to see Your goodness, strength and provision in every situation. Align ___'s heart with Your truth. Bind ___ to Your hope so that this child can joyfully anticipate the fulfillment of Your promises.

FOR TIME WITH
Your CHILD

ASK: Is there any place in your life where you are feeling a little bit discouraged or hopeless? Talk about it together. What do you think God would say about the situation?

PRAY: *I want to be the most hope-filled person alive! Jesus, thank You that because of You, I have a reason to hope, no matter what.*

DECLARE: Hope in God will never disappoint me! I look forward to His love and kindness every day.

DO: If God built a Hope Castle, what would it look like? Build or draw a castle of hope together. As a prophetic act, place the area of your life in which you have experienced some disappointment inside the castle walls.

27

The Person of Peace

"Glory to God in the highest, and on earth peace" (Luke 2:14 NASB). That is the will of God. Peace is that prevailing substance of the atmosphere of heaven. It is the Prince of Peace who crushes the powers of darkness under our feet (see Romans 16:20). Peace is not the absence of noise, conflict or war. It is the presence of Someone. Peace is a Person. It is the abiding presence of the Spirit of God in our lives.

In the Kingdom, you can be in the middle of war and still have peace. This is not the result of mind over matter, but the result of a shift in our perception when we begin to see the way Jesus sees.

We cannot lose our peace in the sense that God abandons us; He never does. But we can lay aside our felt awareness of Him. His peace belongs to us, so if we are feeling anxiety or fear, we can backtrack in our day and figure out where we exchanged our peace for a lie. We have to repent, confess our sin, pick up our peace and realize that it is our permanent possession. The enemy has already been defeated.

An atmosphere of peace is an important building block of a healthy home. Atmosphere is a presence-based value. That means that as parents and grandparents, we get to be intentional about hosting the Spirit of God in our homes. His presence is our greatest treasure. Adoration and affection for Him draw Him close. The atmosphere of our homes and workplaces comes under the influence of our affection for the living God. Learning how to live with that supreme value is paramount to having a home of peace.

The Lord longs to express who He is through His people—His own nature, the way He functions, His beauty and glory. All of that flows through a yielded believer when he or she is free of anxiety and stress. Jesus illustrated that it is possible to live in perfect peace. Think about it: He went to the cross while giving thanks.

For MEDITATION

The LORD will give [unyielding and impenetrable] strength to His people; the LORD will bless His people with peace. *Psalm 29:11 AMP*

Now may the Lord of peace Himself continually grant you peace in every circumstance. The Lord be with you all! *2 Thessalonians 3:16 NASB*

I leave the gift of peace with you—my peace. Not the kind of fragile peace given by the world, but my perfect peace. Don't yield to fear or be troubled in your hearts—instead, be courageous! *John 14:27*

Thank You, Jesus, that You promised to leave Your perfect peace with us. Thank You that Your peace is not fragile; it is strong and empowering. Help ___ and me experience the reality of Your peace throughout the day, Holy Spirit. If I lose my peace, help me go back to where I put it down and picked up fear or anxiety. Help me teach ___ to do the same. We need Your unyielding strength, Lord. We need to be reminded that You paid for everything at the cross and that the enemy has been completely defeated. Help ___ and me see the world as You do.

ASK: Do you ever feel anxious? What helps you feel peaceful?

PRAY: *Thank You, Jesus, that peace is a gift from You. Whenever I get scared, help me wrap up in Your love and peace so that my mind and heart are totally protected.*

DECLARE: I am wrapped up in God's peace like a blanket. Peace protects me like a shield. Fear cannot get past God's love!

DO: Find your favorite gentle song and spend some time resting quietly in God's perfect peace. Pay attention to what His peace feels like in your body.

28

Seated at His Table

Jesus came to make it possible for our sins to be forgiven. In addition to that supreme objective, He had another mission: He came to reveal the Father. And in revealing the Father, He revealed who we are and who God meant for us to be.

When we are born into a family, we are given a name. Our last name reveals our family history and gives our children and grandchildren identity for their future. When Jesus taught the disciples to pray, He said, "Our Father . . . Your kingdom come" (Matthew 6:9–10 NASB). We have been adopted into a Kingdom with a Father. We have been named by the God who has always been, and has always been perfect. Our being named as sons and daughters of the King reveals our nature, our destiny and our purpose.

Romans 8:15 says we have "received the Spirit of adoption by whom we cry out, 'Abba, Father'" (NKJV). This was the purpose of Christ coming to earth. Our planet is filled with orphaned people competing to get ahead and performing for acceptance.

Jesus came to restore the orphaned to God's abundant table, where they no longer have to fight, manipulate and deceive to receive a meal.

Outside Christ, people perform to create an identity so they might be accepted. The longing of everyone's heart is to belong. It is vital. But in Christ, things are different. We start out already accepted by God. From the place of acceptance, our identity is formed. And it is out of our identity that we perform.

When we model and teach that approach to life, it will enable our children to skip years of unnecessary crisis and engage fully with who God made them to be. Being accepted and valued by God the Father is worth the sacrifice of everything else in the world. We have a Father who fixes every pain and provides every meal. There is more than enough for each of us. He has given us His Spirit in unlimited measure, and with that Spirit inside us, our spirit cries out with confidence, "Papa God!"

For MEDITATION

Look with wonder at the depth of the Father's marvelous love that he has lavished on us! He has called us and made us his very own beloved children. The reason the world doesn't recognize who we are is that they didn't recognize him. Beloved, we are God's children right now; however, it is not yet apparent what we will become. But we do know that when it is finally made visible, we will be just like him, for we will see him as he truly is. *1 John 3:1–2*

So God created mankind in his own image, in the image of God he created them; male and female he created them. *Genesis 1:27 NIV*

But you are a chosen generation, a royal priesthood, a holy nation, His own special people, that you may proclaim the praises of Him who called you out of darkness into His marvelous light.

1 Peter 2:9 NKJV

God, I need to sow this truth of my identity as Your child deeply in my heart. Thank You that You see every part of me—my weaknesses, my fears, my strengths— and You call me Yours. Thank You that You have a big table, with more than enough for my family and me. I know You will continue to lavish Your love on us, Father, because we are Your kids. I know Your hand is on ___'s life, guiding, protecting and providing for this child of Yours. __ has been created in Your image, given Your name and called Your child. I trust You with ___'s life and destiny, God. You are such a good Father.

ASK: Close your eyes and imagine you are with Jesus in your favorite place on earth (made-up or real). Now ask Him, *What do You love about me?* What kinds of things come to mind that you think He might say?

PRAY: *Thank You, Jesus, that I can be a child of God. Help me remember that You see and love every part of who I am. I am loved and valued!*

DECLARE: I am God's treasure. There is more than enough for me!

DO: Draw a self-portrait. On your drawing, write out the words and phrases that you heard from Jesus when you asked Him what He loves about you. (Have someone help you with the writing part, if needed.) What are some of the things He loves about you?

29

Taking Up the Towel

Jesus, the King of all glory, came to earth to serve people and minister to them. The disciples had seen Jesus walk on water, feed thousands and heal everyone who came to Him. There wasn't any problem that could prevent Him from displaying the will of God. Jesus was the King, and they expected Him to establish a dominant kingdom on the earth.

Instead, the Bible tells us this: "Jesus, knowing that the Father had given all things into His hands, and that He had come from God and was going to God, rose from supper and laid aside His garments, took a towel and girded Himself" (John 13:3–4 NKJV). In this moment, when Jesus was fully aware of His identity as the Son of God who would be returning to the throne room, He put a towel over His arm and washed the disciples' feet.

Healings and deliverances had illustrated God's Kingdom before their eyes throughout the gospels. But until this moment, the disciples had missed the heart of it all. The King of kings, the one everyone is supposed to serve, began to model what His

Kingdom is truly like: "The greatest among you will be your servant" (Matthew 23:11 NIV).

This moment recalibrated everything for the disciples, as it does for us. We teach serving by doing it, just as Jesus did. The role of the servant is the highest in God's Kingdom. In training our children, it is critical that we illustrate that role before their eyes. As parents and grandparents, we owe them exposure to meeting the needs of people who will never be able to pay us back.

Confidence arises in our children and grandchildren when they know who they are in the Lord. We want them to be secure in their royal identity, willingly taking risks for the Kingdom. But on the journey of identity, some people begin to become impressed with themselves. Understanding our identity is crucial, whereas entitlement just means that we have not truly seen our God. The Father longs for us to see what He is truly like, because then we will leave His presence not impressed with ourselves, but with an extreme confidence that we can serve well.

For MEDITATION

Beloved ones, God has called us to live a life of freedom in the Holy Spirit. But don't view this wonderful freedom as an opportunity to set up a base of operations in the natural realm. Freedom means that we become so completely free of self-indulgence that we become servants of one another, expressing love in all we do. *Galatians 5:13*

For even the Son of Man did not come to be served, but to serve, and to give His life a ransom for many. *Mark 10:45 NKJV*

Each of you should use whatever gift you have received to serve others, as faithful stewards of God's grace in its various forms. *1 Peter 4:10 NIV*

Jesus, You came to bring us freedom and restoration with the Father, but I never want that to turn into entitlement. Help me see opportunities to pick up the towel and serve in my community and in my family. God, I need Your wisdom with ___. I want to raise children who know who and whose they are, and from that place become servants of one another. Help me model Your servant's heart to ___. Help me expose this child safely to the human need that is around us. Expand the compassion of our hearts for others, Lord, so that we can look more and more like You every day.

FOR TIME WITH
Your CHILD

ASK: Have you ever seen someone who needed something that he or she could not get? Maybe the person was homeless, hungry or hurting in some way. How did that make you feel?

PRAY: *Jesus, I want to be Your hands and feet on the earth. Help me serve the people around me with love and compassion.*

DECLARE: I serve others generously! Jesus empowers me to help the people around me.

DO: Think of one practical way you can serve your family or your neighbors today. Maybe it is taking someone a meal, picking up trash on your walk or helping a neighbor with yard-work. Have fun being the hands and feet of Jesus!

30

Safely in His Presence

Our homes are meant to be places of safety and refuge. Life is not fair, and not everyone will be considerate of our children and grandchildren. But our homes get to be places of safety where every family member returns to be strengthened and empowered for the next day. We provide a place of safety for our children and grandchildren, and God provides a shelter of protection over us.

The Bible says, "He who dwells in the shelter of the Most High will abide in the shadow of the Almighty" (Psalm 91:1 NASB). We are meant to dwell in God's presence as a lifestyle. This is not a point of theology, but is rather a conscious awareness of the abiding presence of the Holy Spirit. When we dwell as a family in His presence in this way, we are abiding in His protection. God's presence overshadows us, pulling us into His realm of safety. Corrie ten Boom once said, "When you are covered by His wings, it can get pretty dark." The moment may be dark, but it is only a testament to His nearness.

God is not intimidated by anything. We don't want to shame anyone, especially children, if they are feeling fear, but we can throw them a lifeline of hope. As children of God, we have been called to be an influence in the midst of difficulty and calamity. We are not the answer, but we usher in the answer through the wonderful message of the Gospel.

When Israel was wandering through the desert, God would manifest as a cloud covering in the heat of the day, to bring coolness. In the cold of the night, He was there as a pillar of fire. God shows up opposite of His surroundings. He shows up as the redemptive solution to every problem. In every hellish situation, Jesus has predetermined to redeem every aspect into the promotion of the Gospel. He does not bring calamity, but He is prepared to reverse its effects.

For MEDITATION

He will keep you from every form of evil or calamity as he continually watches over you. You will be guarded by God himself. You will be safe when you leave your home and safely you will return. He will protect you now, and he'll protect you forevermore! *Psalm 121:7–8*

The LORD is good, a refuge in times of trouble. He cares for those who trust in him. *Nahum 1:7 NIV*

My God, my rock, in whom I take refuge, my shield and the horn of my salvation, my stronghold and my refuge; my savior, You save me from violence. *2 Samuel 22:3 NASB*

You are my rock, God! Thank You that whenever I am afraid, I can run into Your arms and take refuge there. You are a shield around us, and You will always be a safe place for ___ and for me. Thank You that You will keep ___ from every form of evil, because You continually watch over ___'s every move. Thank You that I don't need to worry, because You are the Protector over ___ and over my entire family. We invite Your presence to fill our home, overshadowing our family with the wings of Your protection. We trust in You completely.

FOR TIME WITH
Your CHILD

ASK: What makes you feel really safe?

PRAY: *You are my Protector, God, the one I can run to anytime I am afraid. Thank You that You care about every part of my life.*

DECLARE: I am always safe in the arms of my Father God! He watches over me, so I never need to be afraid.

DO: The Bible says God is our shield. Make or draw a shield of His protection over your life.

31

The Gift of Children

Jesus cherished children. Twice, He is recorded teaching about the benefits of receiving them—that is, about accepting, valuing and celebrating them in our lives. The first time, He said, "Whoever receives one of these little children in My name receives Me; and whoever receives Me, receives not Me but Him who sent Me" (Mark 9:37 NKJV). So many of our Christian songs, sermons and prayers focus on our longing for the presence of God, and rightly so. But here, Jesus gives us a shortcut. He draws a direct connection between receiving children and receiving the Father.

Taking time for children is receiving God. When we treasure what He treasures, He takes it personally. Perhaps the "more of Him" that we long for is found in the greater measure in which we receive children.

The second time Jesus teaches about receiving children, He holds them up as the models for receiving and entering into His Kingdom (see Mark 10:14–15). God's Kingdom is the realm of

His dominion, so it stands to reason that the measure in which we receive children is the measure in which we enter His rule, tasting of the benefit of His Kingdom. Our heart's cry is for His world. And amazingly, we enter it through this unusual door called "welcoming and celebrating children into our lives."

Kids are naturally curious, laugh easily, live in a constant state of wonder, forgive quickly and trust openly. Perhaps because of these traits, Jesus calls them the greatest in His Kingdom (see Matthew 18:4). God's Kingdom is filled with extremes of beauty and wonder, excellence and heroes. Yet astonishingly, the greatest in that lineup are children.

Adults are not excluded from this honor, however. The beauty of Jesus' definition of greatness is that everyone can attain it. Greatness in His Kingdom is found in protecting our childlikeness—staying humble, letting our hearts be moved easily with delight, trusting God in all things. In God's Kingdom, significance is not based on gifts or talents; it is found in possessing greatness of heart. That kind of childlikeness is worth fighting anything and everything to maintain.

Children are God's love-gift; they are heaven's generous reward. Children born to a young couple will one day rise to protect and provide for their parents. Happy will be the couple who has many of them! A household full of children will not bring shame on your name but victory when you face your enemies, for your offspring will have influence and honor to prevail on your behalf! *Psalm 127:3–5*

You have built a stronghold by the songs of babies. Strength rises up with the chorus of singing children. This kind of praise has the power to shut Satan's mouth. Childlike worship will silence the madness of those who oppose you. *Psalm 8:2*

Grandchildren are the crowning glory of the aged. *Proverbs 17:6 NLT*

Thank You, Jesus, that You have blessed me with the precious presence of children in my life. You have infused a gift from heaven into my home, and I want to cherish the children under my influence with the same value and honor that You do. Holy Spirit, open my eyes to the childlikeness that ___ carries. Help me learn from ___'s posture of wonder and trust. I want to be this child's greatest source of encouragement. Help me stop and take time for children, as You did, Jesus. Help me spend precious time with ___. Help me speak out the wonderful things I see about ___'s unique personality.

ASK: Did you know that children are very important and special to Jesus? What kind of things make you feel really special?

PRAY: *Thank You, God, that You always have time for me. I am Your precious treasure, and You love spending time with me.*

DECLARE: I am a gift from heaven! I can run into Jesus' arms anytime I want.

DO: What do you like about how God made you? How are you a gift from God to His world? (Take some time to tell the child or children with you, in detail, the things that delight you about who they are.)

BILL and BENI JOHNSON are the senior leaders of Bethel Church in Redding, California. Bill is a fifth-generation pastor with a rich heritage in the Holy Spirit. The present move of God has brought him into a deeper understanding of the phrase "on earth as it is in heaven." Heaven is the model for their life and ministry. Bill and the Bethel Church family have taken on this theme for life and ministry, where healing and miracles are normal. He teaches that we owe the world an encounter with God, and that a gospel without power is not the

Gospel Jesus preached. Bill is also the cofounder of Bethel School of Supernatural Ministry (BSSM).

Beni is a pastor, author and speaker. She has a call to joyful intercession that is an integral part of Bethel Church. Her insight into strategies for prayer and her involvement in prayer networks bring breakthrough with global impact. She is passionate about health and wholeness—in body, soul and spirit.

Together, Bill and Beni serve a growing number of churches that have partnered for revival. This apostolic network has crossed denominational lines in building relationships that enable church leaders to walk in both purity and power. And as Bill says in the pages of the book *Raising Giant-Killers*, home is the beginning point for having that kind of worldwide impact: "Success at home gives us the authority base to go anywhere else . . . it starts at home."

Bill and Beni's goal at home has always been to raise giant-killers through intentional parenting. Their three children are now married and are all serving with their spouses in full-time ministry. Between them, they have given Bill and Beni eleven grandchildren, who are also being raised on God's promises as they grow into a generation of giant-killers.